Acacia Road

The Gerald Cable Book Award Series

Love Fugue
Shulamith Wechter Caine

Dime Store Erotics
Ann Townsend

Bodies that Hum
Beth Gylys

Inventing Difficulty
Jessica Greenbaum

Why They Grow Wings
Nin Andrews

Odd Botany
Thorpe Moeckel

A Parade of Hands
James Hoch

Lime
Audrey Bohanan

Any Holy City
Mark Conway

The Deepest Rooms
Randolph Thomas

Sleeping Upside Down
Kate Lynn Hibbard

What Kills What Kills Us
Kurt S. Olsson

The Odds of Being
Daneen Wardrop

Blue to Fill the Empty Heaven
Joel Friederich

Best Western and Other Poems
Eric Gudas

The Lessons
Joanne Diaz

Close By
Gigi Marks

The Invented Child
Margaret MacKinnon

Bastard Heart
Raphael Dagold

Winter Garden
Robert Hunter Jones

Where Is North
Alison Jarvis

Acacia Road

Aaron Brown

Silverfish Review Press
Eugene, Oregon

Cover art: *Red Desert Sunset* © 2015 by Peggy Hinaekian

Rodger Moody was the 2016 GCBA final judge.

Published by
Silverfish Review Press
PO Box 3541
Eugene, OR 97403
www.silverfishreviewpress.com

Distributed by
Small Press Distribution
800-869-7553
spd@spdbooks.org
www.spdbooks.org

Library of Congress Cataloging-in-Publication Data

Names: Brown, Aaron, 1990- author.
Title: Acacia road / by Aaron Brown.
Description: First edition. | Eugene, Oregon : Silverfish Review Press, 2018. | Poems.
Identifiers: LCCN 2017042993 | ISBN 9781878851697 ("pbk." : alk. paper)
Subjects: | LCGFT: Poetry.
Classification: LCC PS3602.R64874 A6 2018 | DDC 811/.6--dc23
LC record available at https://lccn.loc.gov/2017042993

9 8 7 6 5 4 3 2 First Printing
Printed in the United States of America

Contents

Part III

For Madri Abdel-Aziz

paix à son âme

In those early amorphous years when memory had only just begun, when life was full of Beginnings and no Ends, and Everything was Forever...

—Arundhati Roy

I lost two cities, lovely ones. And, vaster,
some realms I owned, two rivers, a continent.

—Elizabeth Bishop

I say how can we be happy when we are mere wanderers without a home?

—Helon Habila

Acacia Road

Part I

N'Djamena Morning

Mornings like this, the sun shining in patches through the trees—
    the trees with needle-thin leaves

and Moussa tuning the radio...
                                        (crackling)
                                                adjusting the antenna wire

stretching from the box to the metal window grate.

Outside a motorcycle rides by, a lizard brushes across the wall,
    and from on high, the wind makes the topmost mango leaves speak.

Je chante à la radio... et on dit le premier gaou
    n'est pas gaou.

Juliette is digging in the corner of the yard,
    sticking her snout out and breathing in the earth—

she smells the scent of a hedgehog that passed by in the night
    on its way to the road
                                    where the faded Peugeot taxis

        shudder over bumps.

Je savais chanter un peu.

On walks through the neighborhood
    where the tall whitewashed walls of the UN compound

stand silent, it takes some time before you see a human being:
    a uniformed guard, who invites you to sit down
                                                        on his blue stringed chair.

From far off, the sound of a distorted voice comes closer—
    a camouflaged truck kicks up a cloud
                                                and a soldier stands in its bed,

lifts the megaphone to his lips, reminds you of the curfew at ten.

Et on dit...

A chameleon slowly crawls its way across the road,
feels the rumble of an approaching car,

sees the treads with its sideways eye.

The chameleon sticks out its tongue, puffs out its chest,

the back tire
obliterates the tongue.

Je savais chanter un peu. I knew how to sing a little.

Batha River

They say this land was once an ocean, but I have not found the shells
to prove it. The dry riverbed slithers like the trail

of a prehistoric snake, its scales leaving the ruts and cracks along the bank,
dried and caked, sandstoned by sun and drought.

As a child I came to it, the Batha. I saw a sea of dunes dimpling the surface,
saw a train of pack animals exposed under the hot season sun,

hooves treading grains like water, fording the absent river at a snoring
pace—the scratch and rasp of foliated bone on sand,

groan of wood bundles tied against their blistered backs. Their journey
was endless, as a boy's eyes would make it seem, seeing

their trajectory up a hill and through twisted thorn trees to villages
I would never go. But I would return some years later,

a few years older, when the clouds emptied like a jug, drops birthed by harmattan
wind, my friends and I traversing bog and bird-trees,

standing under the mighty haraza, a tree so tall the clouds settled in its leaves,
the branches marked the four winds. In its roots, we found

stones brought from the depths of earth, shaped by a thousand years of ocean,
warmed by desert sun and our eager hands.

We had waited three months to hear the news: to hear of it coming, coming
from the southern lake swelled by rain, turning

and overturning the dunes and rocks and roots, sand turned to mud
turned to liquid, risen three feet then ten, the villagers

waiting with fish lines, rushing the word faster downstream than the water rose.
My friends heard the news on market day, brought it through

my door, and so we came, stones in hand, coiling out our wrists in unison.
We threw them: a skip, a second, a third, submerged.

Twin

He had invited me over for coffee, and so we sat
sipping clear glasses—the way he always made it
syrup-sweet, sludge-thick so that it burns the throat.

We sat in his one-room mud house, on a flowered rug
shuttled across oceans and deserts to reach us
on the Saharan edge, windswept and forgotten.

I watched him heat coals in a brazier, place them
in an iron and hover his hand over its surface,
judge it ready to press fresh clothes.

I watched as he spread his shirt across the rug,
brush it with heat until it lost its wrinkles,
then fold it with a hand, his only good hand,

which had survived a botched birth, broken
in his brother's wake and set by a marabout
tying it too tight with unskilled hands—

the arm still twisted eighteen years later,
a reminder of the mother who died giving him life
and the brother, unblemished, whose prospects

are as clear as the skies emptied of kharrif rain
when his own cloud over, doomed to watch others
drive the herds out in the morning or mount

market trucks as hired hands. I know he irons
every Saturday. He sprinkles water on a pair of pants,
picks up the iron, brings it down, presses and repeats.

Motorcycle at Maghrib

You had called me before prayertime to see if we would go out,
a guys' night on the town, and so you came, the knockoff Honda roaring

underneath the stars, headlight a single bulb barely stronger than a flashlight,
illuminating every chipped brick and bounce of rut along the road

from the clinic (that used to be the edge of town) toward the city center,
where fluorescents form a dusty halo in the dark, an ethereal glow that guides

us there, guides us to it. I said *Don't drive too fast* as we left and you only
laughed, talking me through the streets that night, past the silent gates

where I had entered so long ago. *That is Bichara's home, do you remember?*

Was the big mosque here when you left?

At the restaurant, you were the host, the life of the party, finding us a table
on the streetside, ordering the top three things on the menu: an omelette,

steaming nashif, and bread barely stale at the end of the day. We gorged
ourselves as we talked about life after five years' absence—

You gave me that shirt, do you remember?
The one with number 41 on it, the Nowitzki shirt. I never

wear it. I leave it in the corner of my room
so that it never fades or tears.

The food nearly gone, you smacked your lips and snapped at the waiter boy
until he brought us a round of mango smoothies. The cool grit and sweet sank

down our throats, drawing us into silence as we watched the previously
nonexistent nightlife bustle down the main road: buyers of phone credit,

Nigerian cigarettes, and bus tickets for those new twenty-seaters that rumble
six hundred miles to the east, ceiling lights revealing bag-eyed passengers

clutching their belongings close to chest—wary of petty thieves even in sleep.
Let's leave, you said, so we got on the moto one last time, riding back to what

used to be the edge of town, and sometimes in crisp twilight, when constellations
emerge, I'm almost convinced the motorcycle still hums, still goes beyond
the furthest light.

Teacher

for Oustaz Boukhari

That evening we shared a bowl of assir, like honey
the guava nectar so cold the metal clouded around

the chalk dust left by your fingertips. You had just
finished a lecture, somewhere down the street, teaching

the youth how to speak, how to read, how to think
before they left to till their fathers' fields out of town.

But behind your door, my brother and I took in your mind,
there in the diminishing afternoon, you so tired you could only

drink juice and crack jokes that danced around the intricacies
of Arabic, the tin door rattling with every gust of dust

as the cows come into town—we heard them call out
their arrival, the gentle rumble of their hooves on sand,

the close coming of each one down the street and into the houses
of neighbors, to the same corner of yard where they spend

every night, where a bowl of hay waits by the tetherpole,
for slow chewing through the hours.

Ramadan

In dust season December, we rolled out our rugs at Ramadan,
filled the beige thermos (don't drink!) over the inscribed mat, *Ramadan.*

Friends filtering in like slivers of window light, we broke out
a new pack of Bicycle playing cards, saved just for that Ramadan.

In humid November, the short bearded plumber stepped
from the Sudanese bus, tools in hand—that fall we met Ramadan.

The hardest worker, sweat beads sliding down his forearm,
shirt soaked, he wouldn't have a drop of water: *It's Ramadan.*

The hottest August, dear friend Mahamat wouldn't stop dribbling
the basketball, so long as he could find a spot and spit (Ramadan).

At the end of day, an hour still left to Maghrib, he'd take up
the ball in the curl of his fingers, find and hit the net, Ramadan.

Under the summer sun, July sky dimpled with cloud, the old men
of Sultanahmet lit cigarettes and didn't give a flip about Ramadan.

They didn't seem to care, they didn't seem to remember the brown
summer laughter and long-hour sweltering wait of Ramadan.

Song of the Workers

Before the sun rises, I hear the shovels out in the corner of the yard, scraping.
Clément, the leader of the bunch, sets the tune of some sorrowful song

of the south: first the hum and then the words, the words that escape his lips—
a song of the grandmother who made him boulle, who made him sit

and sop the sauce with its grittiness in his fingers. The song of the ferry
crossing the Logone—he remembers the day as a young boy

his father took him by the hand, cigarette steeping in the mouth,
and together they rode a 14-seater north.

When they reached the outskirts of the truckstop market, young Clément
watched city boys parade around the van windows, selling radios,

batteries and chewing gum for the clink of a few coins in their beggars' cups,
and this was just the market's start. When they came to

his father's cousin's house in Moursal, his father took up the hammer
and never left the square space of yard, always pounding and planing

long slender slabs of Cameroonian timber. Within a day he could build a table:
legs arched on the side, finishes ornate, and then he'd sit back

in his rope-strung chair (the ropes unraveling) and sip marrissay till his eyes
shut, the sawdust settling in his beard, and Clément crawling up

his father's knee to pluck from his chin what he thought was gold.

Sakina

Your brother was having another naming ceremony for another child,
    and after we had all heard the faki speak and the name

of the child whispered from man to man, we sipped tea together
    and you wondered what my sadikti was like,

how she was far away, and whether she would become my wife—
    and she did, but you would no longer be alive to see, only

we sat sipping, and sometimes in my thoughts I wander back
    to the same mat, to the same morning, to the same

sound of you whispering in my ear your new niece's name, *Sakina,*
    meaning *peace,* meaning *serenity,* meaning *rest,*

and how could I have known, that before all of us, before your
    aging mother and drunk of a brother, you would find it first?

Maternal

when I see you again
    what will we say

    to each other
my Chadian grandmother

you brought me
    spiced and steaming coffee

    you made me sit and drink
your eyes proud of who

I was becoming
    a *rajil* you said so emphatically

    the same eyes with which
you gazed at your blood-son

your youngest given to you
    in husband's memory

    conceived before they took your love
and shot him at the outskirts

your Madri would grow
    to care for you in old age

    to provide for his brothers
who couldn't keep a job

for drink and lounging around
    but he was taken too

    dead from his motorcycle
and what must you say

to the shriveled tree
    in your backyard

the one under which you sit
    pouring coffee for guests

serving them sweet biscuits and dates

During Kharrif

We held the mangos in our hands,
the skin ripe and firm, and sliced
until we had a plateful of gold.

We puffed out our bellies as if pregnant
and laughed, talking politics and soccer
over glasses of mango juice.

Outside, rainy season winds scattered
twigs and hajlij seeds across the earth,
a thickened cloud hovered like soot

over the horizon, threatening to spill its
entrails upon the leaves outside my door.
The yard would erode, bricks disintegrate

in a wash of sand and rain—a deluge
that could not drown the whir of the blender,
the scoop of spoons in the sugar jar.

N'Djamena, Meaning 'We Will Rest'

The day the looters broke into our house was the shot fired
as my father yelled and the fear that came with the window

darkened by the men looking in and the scuffing of sandals on
a packed-dirt yard, the grind of metal loosened, the voices

between walls, the bullet that never came, and the hack job that
never was by a drunken soldier wielding a machete under-

oiled and overused on thickets by roads and rows of bodies.
I waited for an execution like at my friend's house two years

before when a rebel was found hiding and forced to kneel,
a bullet to his brain. I waited against the wall seeking flatness,

transparency, hoping the shadows never recede. This was the end
of going to bed with no thought of fear, the beginning of chilled

sweats, the beginning of sounds signaling the departure of a place
once known—the sound of curtains riding wind, ceiling fans beating

air, the sound of opened bags and belongings strewn across the floor,
of receding taillights and a street littered with empty shells.

Memory Palace

Let us implore that it be returned to us,
That second space.
—Milosz

In my father's house, there are rooms where I might wander,
finding in each the rubble of childhood—a reading chair,
maroon rug, cluttered toys—things on which I could
place a memory, if only I could return—

return to search the worn spines of books with talking mice,
trace Arabic calligraphy with untrained eyes and speak
the words of a language primer: *Ghitatti sakhira, ismaha Samira.*
I could cover these covers with a thought I never wish to lose.

Each room would be a category—in one, the cabinet of drawers
housing a friend who found a gun in his father's car, the car in which
he drove the sheikh, and the father who found his son's blood on the seat.
In my schoolroom, the desk over which the owls clawed in the rafters

where I project the time I hunted with a sling birds the size of my thumb,
and found none. An unstrung bow to remind me of the afternoons
when I couldn't mark the words, couldn't say, *How is your health?*
Will you be back tomorrow? The time I was promised he would return,

but he never did and something was missing from my toys,
a bright green gun. A bright green gun to remind me of the trucks
burdened with soldiers speeding off to the eastern front, leaving
a wake of dust only too eager to rise. And how could I forget

the dust that rests on every countertop and crevice, chair and shoe?
The particles raised by the mortar and pestle beating to the smoke
of cookfires, dust settling on my bed, in a closet, down a hall where
I articulate all memories into one: a toy gun, unstrung bow,

desk with owl feathers, cabinet spilling blood, the spines of books
I never had the time to read. If I lose the way back to this place,
lose it at a wrong turn and into a wrong room, it will not be for lack
of things to stand in place of other things, but for the will to look.

Part II

Aubade

In the spacious halls of morning, beneath the wind-lifted curtain,
I played a song on a three-string harp before the waking hours.

Was it there that I first found you—where the wind coming in
brought the first raindust and outside Amin swept the yard

with a broom that reached only to his knee? Or were you
in the wind that shook so loudly that the seeds of the hajlij tree

fell and pocked the sand beneath? Were you in the seeds
themselves, fruit burst like skin surrounding the dry and bitter pit?

I do not know where to find you. I do not know
how to find my way back to that place.

I wake before the sun has risen, wake and walk out
to the wicker chairs outside my door, but you are not

there in the silence. You are not underneath the wicker chairs
nor are you behind the shoulder-high shrubs. You are not

in the breaking sky, blood-rushed till morning. There is a path
stretching out in the dying dark, through a field of saltgrass

and rabbit holes, and only I am here alone to say to you, *Listen,*
listen closely—listen to the three-string harp once again.

Acacia Road

From thirteen thousand feet, the twisting acacias—thirsty thorn-trees reaching
a web of fingers up to the sky, into the earth—look like shrubs

shriveled under the sun seeming so distant, yet so present with its heat.
Streams of cattle ridge like ocean waves across the plains, the sleek

and sheen of their backs, ants' exoskeletons, labor for miles
to the burst of brush beyond the endless nagga. Rising from earth

mountains pepper the plain: mounds of rocks, marbles of God, pile high
above dom trees whose black seeds clump like fistfuls of obsidian—

when they fall they make the sound of a bullet rushing through a dust devil,
rushing to the point of impact in the sand silencing

the sound of lead. From thirteen thousand feet, I wonder if a shepherd
roaming the road remembers the rebel trucks that breathed death

into the dust, clouding air with sandgrain, cloaking black barrels of kalashes
aimed across a land I now study, five years later through the plexiglass,

a land sucked dry, flying to the town at the world's edge, the place no soldier
would go. The circles of huts and thatch swell as the empty oxbows

wind a road to follow—a road that breaks at carcasses of colonial homes,
empty at town's edge, and the huts that become mud roofs sinking

like worn mattresses, surrounded by ruts weaving between rows of homes
and people streaming in polyester gold and deep azure sky—

and somewhere, down there, a three-part gate along chari kabir stands
as the entry to mine, but to find it, turn at the broken cement mixer,

the one left lying abandoned by a truck traversing the desert so far it makes
light its load, casting off the disrepaired, losing its cargo piece by piece.

Aviate

That moment
when wings

break upon
up-rushing currents

Sahel-wind heat
baking dirt-clay

almost as if
the earth resists

your coming.

Picture of a Family

after Cavafy

There's a photo he carries for long journeys
like this one, for trips on loaded market lorries
where passengers take their seats, perching
on top of cargo, or sitting on crude benches
inside the buses coming from Maiduguri with names
like "Best of Luck" or "Mr. Good Looking."

As the road rumbles from Chad through Cameroon
to Nigeria, toward another year of medical school,
he reaches into his inside coat pocket, brings
out the folded 4x6—sees his brother wearing
the latest jeans from the capital and a maroon
hoodie zipped half-way up, one leg placed forward,
head tilted back—*une attitude* he's learned
from movies and music pipelined from America.

Sees his mother, bright pink polyester swirling
around her figure, and remembers how she woke
before dawn to make him fangaso for his trip.
He sees the lines he and his brother have caused,
drawn into her face after years of worry,
husbandless years selling market produce
and begging relatives. He sees the slight
twist of her mouth, slight triumph of a mother
despite another leave-taking, content
with just a promise for a better life.

The Funeral

They have told her Youssouf has left this life, left it on the road
between Ngoura and Amjamena—he fell twice off the hood

where he had been perched, refusing a seat in the cabin
when the third lurch brought him to the earth,

and under the right rear tire. Without the father of her children,
what was she left to do except marry her daughter

to the guard across the street, his impotence rumor's wind—
the reason that within years their marriage was over,

and she let her son enlist (he sends money when he's sober)
and on the day of the death, the yard filled with neighbors

who beat their chests, who screamed so that Allah
might tip the scales in Youssouf's favor. They silenced

to count the ninety-nine names, made it somewhere around
six thousand before the day was done and I could hear

the hush of death stealing like a cloud over the mud wall.
I could not move or go to say the single word *kalawah*—

the word that seems so outside of Arabic it must have been
made up for a day like this when you meet your death

between wheel and sand, and how could I do anything
except pause at the dying of the sun and think of you,

Youssouf, wrapped in seven meters of linen, lowered
into a grave dug in collapsing sand, somewhere

between Ngoura and Amjamena, where a stone the size of a fist
marks your grave, and the shadows it casts mark the hours,

like a dial that disappears at noon, or at night.

I don't know anything about suffering

as in losing three children to a sickness you can't even name,
as in losing your baby boy
five days after birth

while you rode a market truck coming home to see him,
as in saying that a dead child has
returned

rather than *died*
(as if that could make it all easier)

as in riding the back of a motorbike and hitting an acacia tree,
the chain or the wheel snapping your femur,

as in waking every morning to the sound of your children dying

(from whooping cough)

as in walking the fields at noon to glean a bowlful of grain—

how painful when your husband

never returned from the war and the journey he made
across the desert to find a job in Geneina,

to marry the second wife
so much younger,

she didn't bear a stillborn three years in like you—
as if you weren't trying, as if you didn't want to please him

as if every dead and dying thing was
under your control

and you could make the clouds drop rain and breathe life
into a brittle carcass by the roadside,

as if you could even begin to think with a mind that for once
wasn't parched as in the road you walk to your field

every morning, several kilometers away,
                                        joining with the others

who bear the same blows, wear the same cracks, who sweep
  the endless horizon with their eyes and reach

          their jagged arms

to the single cloud that won't let go, won't seal up earth's scars,

                              though everyone asks it why.

Rush

In the vastness between Fitri and Ati, some lucky soul
first strikes gold in a sandhole

holding the speck up
so that the light might verify its gild apart from grit—and he takes a picture

that within hours is shared from Ambassatna to OumHadjer and the diggers
come:
alighting from dust-drenched Toyotas, tossing rusted shovels to earth

they begin their work:

first, scraping away the hardened clay till the plain's
encasement turns to clod—which scrutinized closely, reveals the gold gleam

within quartzite stone, which leads to more shoveling, feverish and focused
on the virgin earth breaking up before them.

Some begin the sifting
through the metal screen colanders borrowed from their wives:

sand winnowed down to scattered grain till gold specks
rattle across screen mesh like light-beat symbols, serenading

their labor—and shout! from here, from there, the plain bursts
voices caught by the four winds, which only proves
to spread the news further

which brings nomads, villagers, pilgrims—even the wealthy boss men
from town—and carrying up their back, the cobra-colored soldier trucks.

They are ruthless—guns spewing goldfire from nozzle,
bodies falling into the trenches and holes just carved.

The soldiers only stopping
to keep the corpses out

of the holes they'll step into themselves, minutes later.

Gazelle

teach me
the balance

between
two spheres

the weave
through

root & rock
& sky

when turbaned
soldiers

aiming AKs
come in camo

trucks
teach me

speed's secret—
the burst

to launch
from this

earth patch
to the next

Train à Grande Vitesse

Somewhere, somehow it's shuttling past,
the metals humming, windows lulled to sleep
by rushing wind
                                        rushing but only

so long as the train moves,
    to stop would mean silence, the kind one feels

when stepping down on the platform,
and it's late—the hour hand standing straight.
No one is there to meet you.

So you walk out the station, walk along the Seine,
and every postcard image
blazes against the never-setting night.

But you don't have eyes to see it, not that
you'd want to anyway, and you can only think
of the roll-out bed in a banlieue
you need three connections to reach.

You remember then how much you prefer
movement, the movement outside your window
while you sit perfectly still, watching
a man with a pencil moustache eat his lunch,
turning to the next page of the *Monde*.

Mysterious Boats Continue to Arrive on Japanese Coast

Salt spray forms a half-second cloud
    as the ship dips into another

rolling wave before rising to break
    foam-crest. The coastguard hails it

but hears no reply, no voice along
    salt wind, nor sees

bobbing heads to confirm
    men work in its bowels.

So they set down a boarding party,
    three men in a motorized raft

easing alongside the derelict,
    each man looking at another—

and the lead man lets his hand
    linger on the ship's edge

before he pulls himself up
    to see what's inside:

headless body, rotting like beached squid.
    Piled at stern, what looks to be

rocks are three skulls, barnacled,
    sucked clean. It's been this way

for twelve months: ship after ship
    strewn with torn fishing nets,

bodies baking in saline sun, bodies
    so decomposed understanding

death is made difficult: Could flesh-rot
    hide bullet-holes or mask the slash

of an officer's blade? Could execution
    have been quick like a hawk strike—

prey more stunned than dead?
  There were four men in this one,

perhaps young, who struck off
  at first light to cast nets

starboard, thinking they saw the shoreline
  of Honshu rimming horizon,

could reach it before the next day dawned,
  could outrun black-ribbed

clouds brooding over them,
  the fresh-pressed uniforms

of the Pyongyang-ordained:
  those ceremoniously blessed,

commissioned to be fishers of men.

Coming of Age

Along Boulevard du Montparnasse on a Thursday, a protest day,
I walked not knowing my mistake until it was too late

when swarms of university students, a year or so older than me,
swept the street—sirens blared, police took up positions—

and down one alley and then another, I came to them not knowing
what they protested against, only that they stood in my way

from an afternoon walk when I wanted to see something
more than marching feet, upended trash cans.

I tried to cross the swelling boulevard, got caught in the sweep,
an undertow that pulled me side to side and always down

towards the Eiffel Tower looming distant—and looking out
across the raised fists and linked arms, I saw an entrance

to the Metro on my side of the road, dropped down
the stairs and found the crowd there, too, drumming

on metal bars and scaling turnstiles, pushing me up
to the surface. I fled back to my quiet street,

the street named after some mountain, the street
where a bakery stood at its end to hold the masses

from my chip-painted door which drew apart
with a tug of my hand, and clicked together again,

myself inside, down in the basement where the beams held
the centuries-old building together with a groan. I tried

to forget the chants, the fists, the linked arms blocking my way.
That was five years ago, but what about thirteen

when I stood as a boy in Florence and watched a train
of Hare Krishnas come through, an undulating wave

of shaved heads and faces glossed serene—
men and women beating the drum, men and women

dancing and joining their voices in deep-hearted song,
and I could only watch and ask *Who are they?* as their music

flooded the street and took minutes more to fade
as they passed down. I felt the tug to join them, to dance

with abandon as the crowd looked on, but I didn't.
For days, whether in a museum or a bookstore,

scanning the shelves, cup of hot chocolate in hand, I couldn't
think of anything but shaved heads and saffron, sweeping robes.

Maps

Before going out I look up the address on my computer
I see if I can park nearby if there's a toll I can avoid

see if there's a marker that will let me know I'm almost
there but not quite only pay attention

pay attention
                    or you will miss

          your destination

this wasn't how it used to be no not when maps
were only pieces of paper like the one put out

by the bureau des cartes it was only several lines
I could see where the little villages were villages

that were in the wrong place they moved six or seven
times over the decades following

                                        the ephemeral river

creeping closer to wells I'm not sure what I would
have done with this map tacked up to a board

in our storage room I walked by every day until
somehow it ripped and got covered in dust and cobwebs

because we never really looked at it and the board
wound up being used for something else maybe shelves

Jiangxi Citizens See Floating City, Phenomenon Caused by Refracted Light

They pour out into the streets by the thousands, cars parked quiet like
upturned faces—clouds billowing colossal Olympus spume

and from their shadows

the dark fortress of a city hovers heavenward and broods for minutes
in refracted light, a masterpiece matching Miyazaki.

The vision dulls Jiangxi conversation, observers look silent in wonderment,
think to themselves the light will break through, revealing a lie

but still the clouds hold.

A man youthful like me
gazes up and places belief in the portal opening up before him:
highways heaving from some limitless expanse between buildings scraping sky

clean of bluish hue and space darkness lurking beyond—

If only a ladder tall enough,
a pilot brave enough.

What he sees solidifies: floating city becoming mountain rock.
His eyes make the journey to the small square window he knows too well

[Building #32]

on the town's west side where rose petals blossom just as they did this morning
when he left for work, light shafts dancing around single stem.

In tempest current, the flower lets loose a single leaf lifeless along the jet stream,
pitching it to and fro, pale rimmed-rose dipping
and falling.

He utters a prayer—
the petal fades in and out of cloud before it breaks
moisture's undercarriage, careening all directions and down

the last few thousand feet to the dirt that seeded it.
He watches it fall the long way to earth.

The Bird

They brought it from the wetlands around Fitri—
a gray-crowned crane, as tall as I was then,
neck stiffened with muscle, body
built upon stick legs and far on high
the beak, all-seeing eyes, and crest
of gold strands ringing skull rim. The bird
made the patch of yard by the guesthouse
its domain, settling under papaya trees, water
reservoir, gasoline barrels, staring through
the break in the wall to the central
yard where visitors came, drank tea, made
small talk about the new family member, and left.

For the few nights we had it, I crossed
the yard, saw it in the corner, standing,
its bead eyes following my figure.
It was as if the life had been taken out of it—
wouldn't drink, hardly ate—and on the third day,
my friend's face downturned with sadness, Moussa
lifted the death-stiffened bird in dawnlight.

I do not know where he took it.
Maybe he buried it among the papaya roots,
shoots springing from featherweight bones, or—
perhaps this is truer—the bird burned
in the rusted-out hulk of a diesel barrel,
the one we always used to turn trash into ashes:
sparks taking flight, let loose as the full moon
lingers with us and the street children sing to it.

Broken Oud

On the willows there
We hung up our lyres
—Psalm 137

I bought it when I was seventeen along the streets of Amman,
instrument store smelling like pine, humidifiers belching steam.

It rode between my legs on Egypt Air, a child I cradled when changing planes.
In a dark room, once home, I tuned its wooden pegs, cursed as they untuned.

I plucked a few plaintive notes, slid my fingers down its unfretted neck:
I was no Munir Bashir—no notes sounding lament. Mine were first attempts

at hearing how one note slides into another, the call to prayer
meandering between octaves like a trash bag in sandstorm wind,

a scale Mozart never knew. When I crossed oceans, the oud
rode with me again until I found my new home

where I strummed its strings into the night, notes
becoming melodies. But one night, so tired, I lifted myself

into my college loft—forgot its presence there—and woke
to find it on the ground some eight feet down.

When I raised it, the neck, the headstock, the rounded belly
where deep notes dwelled, disintegrated in my hands,

pieces like hourglass grains: the time was up.
It waits in my parents' house, closeted,

zipped-up in a black jacket sleeve. There was a time, like now,
I did not play it. A time, like now, I didn't have it with me—

forgotten in a home I fled because of war.
But I could still hear its rhythms, its music

reached me then, led me to fly three thousand miles
across the middle sea and Libya, brought me home

to find it in an abandoned room, floors dust-covered in a looted house.
I ran my hands around its varnished hull, positioned my fingers

for the first few notes—I played a song of return
I can't remember now. Place the instrument in my hands again.

Watch how my fingers falter.

Nasara

The word the kids would shout gleefully at the white boy walking down
    their street; the same that would make my limbs listless, make me notice

my skin, how it resembled more the sands baked by the sun
    than the warm earth richness of theirs—I wanted to chameleon

my way through the streets without being singled out as *nasara,*
    as foreigner, as other. The word reminded me of what I was not.

The word I did not understand until years later, a man, I leafed
    through the pages of a magazine, saw the same word, *nasara,*

Nazarene, the first of its Arabic letters, *nun,* embossed on the cover page.
    Reading how the letter was painted on the doors of Christians in Iraq,

how militants would come back later to gather the flock and line them up
    above a fresh-dug trench. The same word I read and had to put down

to stare at the blinds, the way they only let in a fraction of light
    even at midday, and I was chilled by the sense of a word

I was hearing as if for the first time, a meaning more for me
    than it ever should have meant—the children only wanting

to see me turn and smile, those around me only wanting me
    to come and rest, to let go my words and let them join with theirs,

to dwell in the shade of language in a place beyond the past, where I sit,
    with glossed pages lying bare and open, reading between their lines

a vision where another boy is taken out into the street, gun to his head,
    all because of that single word, *nasara,* meaning, *believer.*

Village, Tanzania

Here at the edge of the world
or, for others, the center
of the heartland—where
the soot of cookfire smoke
lingers with mountain clouds,
where straggling sheep
graze clumping shoots
and bike-tire shoes circle
tracks across the path
to the hearth-lit speakeasy
at the village heart—here
we walked not touching
each other's hands
for that would make the villagers
talk, but instead we chose quiet,
communing in the dying light,
walking along the path worn
by cloven hooves and human
feet, we who were bundled
in warm-up jackets mid-July
upon a hill in Safwaland.

for MNB

After the return, you try to tell them how it was

to see a friend after five long years, an absence stretching
continents and oceans, tell them how it was to see him

walk into the café beaming, beaming just like the time
he beat you at basketball or the time you stayed up late

with your brother and him watching grade B war films.
He hasn't changed a bit and you set down your tea glass

and laugh yourself into a silence with him, seeing how
perhaps his dimples have deepened and the flecks of gray

in his hair increased, why you call him *father of age*
though he's in his twenties. You realize it's this silence

of time you've missed with him and with others, time
sitting down and sharing everything except words,

speaking in smiles and spending in the currency
of hours—you had no better place to be.

Outside Ngaoundéré

after Dante

While driving above the valley, along a rut
of road, I saw the river dropping into an abyss—
couldn't gaze below for the trees, the thickly woven

curtain of brush and millet stalks, but knowing I must
find a way, must find the place where the falling river
meets the earth, I searched until the gateway revealed

its mouth to me, the break in the growth through which
steam rose. I heard the roar somewhere down
its muddy path, the path I stumbled down for an hour,

slipping on rock and root, sliding when I lost my
footing, sludge chuckling at my feeble attempts
to resist—I hardly had the time to stand before

I saw that I had emerged onto a steep bank,
and there before me was the whirlpool, cloud
of mist that hissed a warning to those who approached,

and its wall of falling water, coming down as if from sky.
I felt my way along the pool's edge, where foam,
once churned, now came to collect on my soaked shoes.

I risked submersion but for the promise of land—
a peninsula breaking out from the cliff, into the roar
of water. Climbing, I crept up this risen island,

this rock of two trees, broken baskets, abandoned shoe;
this rock, metamorphic and lacquered, firmly fixed
in swirls lapping its sides, reaching for my ankles.

In the midst of the steam, the roar, the water
that somehow rained yet remained the same,
I stood and found myself in its center.

The Calling

I

In three days, they took down the temple brick by brick:
the steel-toothed claws ripping apart tile and mortar,

old rusted pipes bursting like shredded paper
while the demolition crew crawled around onsite,

hard hats mirroring the summer sun till the day
when the dark-fisted cloud crept across the July sky—

the rain that followed washed clean the remains
of the unused university building, runoff

streaming down the cracked drains of the last wall.
Wind threatened to collapse the exposed ribcage

of iron beam and ceiling timber, wind across
the sidewalks and through the oaks lining

the expanse of grass, emptied of students on break,
filled with the fog of a tempest so thick I couldn't see

out the barred windows of the library. I waited
for the break in the storm like a cloud

across the sun that seemed to speak, *Leave*
or you'll lose your chance.

II

Outside, the wind had left its rubble along the sidewalk:
branches broken, acorns split, mud washed

along the path like brushstrokes. Fog settled down
and in its break I saw flashes of a place

I had left that wasn't the library or the bus stop
but dunes, thorn trees, carcasses of cows,

and the dry bed of a rahad yet to be filled, and I saw him,
riding on his motorcycle, riding the dirt road he takes

to work every morning, Madri coming from the mist.
We met in between the fog and trees, soaking

in the quiet rain we shared. I had forgotten
the lines across his forehead, forgotten how long

I had tried to make sense of his death. He was dry
and his voice was dry, as if it hadn't been used

these sixteen months in the soil.

III

His words came over the rain patter, light yet labored:
When the last child has died of thirst, when the old woman

goes past the furthest house and disappears in the desert,
when the last bull has withered to its ribs, breathed its final

breath, and the mourners still gather ten years later,
still say my name and sip the same tea on the same rug

in the same yard, when the water never comes again
to the dry riverbed, and it has been dammed upstream,

when all the herdsmen have waited hours
for its drops—who will write about this place?

I said *I will* I said *I have to* and then I walked past.

Part III

Fragment

Mornings like this: far-off howitzer guns at city's edge—
invading dreams first as drums and then
rainstorm splitting thunder.

Endless shelling like falling water—like the break in the brush
you found a year before in Cameroon and the river that emptied

itself into the whirlpool below. You walked the felled tree to stand
underneath its surface, felt your feet slip with each step—

a hundred days before you saw the woman, child in hand, balancing her
belongings in a head-burdened bowl—the woman with the others

at the bridge to Cameroon. A thousand francs and she could cross too.

Into Another Intensity

The elders and maples move faster now—
black oaks brush strokes across fields

until brindled cows are blurred stones,

barns slumbering mountains,
and the road, an oxbow river.

Rush its stream, you who wade into it

every day, not caring. Let it carry the dust
of your body, suspending your bone-silt

until it spits you out on a far shore.

Here you rise to see an empty riverbed,
abandoned boat with a hole the size

of a camel streaming through its upturned hull.

And on the far shore, recognize the figure
of a man you can't quite distinguish,

but know that you know from somewhere.

He returns your gaze with his, turns away his
disappearing body, and follows a path

between the neem trees.

Communion

When you promised you
would return but didn't when
you unlatched the blue door
& looked my way one last
time & said you'd be back
when the others placed a
hand on my shoulder & said
*he's lying he has no intention
of coming again* when I
shook my head & replied *but
he just told me* when I saw
you years later both of us
grown men & you with a new
wife & child when you came
& took a seat by the gum tree
& poured a glass when the
vapor rose from the surface
& I could smell the leaf &
mint when we took slow sips
when the swallows broke
from the neighbor's thatch
roof & were consumed in the
twilight haze—then and only
then could we share a kind of
silence the pause between
one cup of tea & the next.

Elegy

We were supposed
to become old men:

our wives mingling
as friends,

grinding millet
to powder over

the conversation
of stifling afternoons,

and our children
giggling meanwhile,

shooting marbles
and flipping cards—

the games we used to
play not too long ago.

We were supposed
to be two old men,

sharing
in the silence

of empty tea glasses,
laughing at God's humor

instead of just me
wondering

why he'd want you
when I still do.

Elsewhere

One day you searched for memory and found it riding sideways
    in the Metro

catching the scent of a cigarette in Paris
                                        or perhaps Istanbul

(it's these things you can't be sure of anymore)

the air held the same desert grains collecting
    against the N'Djamena curb

where white road-lines fade, where rickety cabs coast
    to filling stations,

where the streetlights hang lifeless for years

                        waiting for repair.

You tried then to make places stand in for those
    that have been lost—

like the time you took the train into Chicago for no other reason
    than to roam the streets at rush hour—

the street drummers drumming the rhythm of the men and women
    returning to the station, and you saw the ghost

of a friend now gone in a break between them,
    before the crowd closed in again   and again

you were left as you always have been, trying to make something
    out of something

                trying

just like the day you searched for God in Salisbury Cathedral,
        climbed through the rafters
                                        to the tip of the spire

climbed even out the bolted windows but didn't see him there,
        until you looked down

and found him in the faces of the people walking the grounds.

Ghazal

Drums sounding from dream-depths, I sleep to keep safe this city,
to keep dreaming I haven't yet feared death, felt the loss of this city.

And waking, ever-present dustlight coming through the screen,
I hear the interminable sound of resounding guns across this city.

I dress as the gun-sounds grow, the curtains playing with the breeze
as if shot by a thousand unseen bullets, filled with the silence of this city.

Outside, the yard is empty, the walls shudder from the waves bullet-sounds
make, and for hours I pray, weighing the delicate balance in this city.

And when the rotors cease their beating, shells scattered across asphalt,
I emerge from the comfort of walls and think I have escaped this city.

From the rooftop, turning and hearing a city's death rattle, I see
the palace billowing, imagine the president conceding his city.

His loss is nothing like his people's—the bricks burned and branches broken
over pavement, mothers leading their daughters away from this place, this city.

And the smoke from the palace signals to me: I am no longer Haroun
but Aaron, marked for earth-wandering, searching for a way back to this city.

Battle of N'Djamena – February 2, 2008

Lake Kivu Dream

Mess of streets and shanties, crossroads of war where masses throng,
faces sunken and hands begging at barred truck windows, the trucks

speeding to camps birthed in blood, the fields fallowed by the flowing lava
and the roads caked molten all the way from the slopes of Nyiragongo

down to the shore where I stand, staring into the lake's depths—waiting for
what I can't say. Only, a vapor rises somnolent, and beneath the lake's layers

somewhere the methane lies limnic, waits under volcano shadow belching cloud
and ash over the paving roads and walls torn by shells and lava and hands

piecing together brick by brick, war's rubble, peace's silence. To which my back
is turned. Somewhere a man wakes up to see his children sleeping, somewhere

he goes outside and sees his neighbors sleeping, somewhere he rides his bike
up to crater ridge and sleeps underneath the jujube tree. Somewhere a troop

of silverbacks circle a termite castle, poking and prodding with the bluntness
of their fingers withdrawing to see bug whiteness and mandibular

henna tattoos. Somewhere green leaves mask green uniforms, hovering
spider-like in cookfire smoke, watching children at play with metamorphic

pebbles, bouncing away the hours in their hands, and somewhere, the lava
has reached the shore, sinking beneath the surface and creeping along

the floor to the million-parts of poison trapped under the gentle waves. I await
the detonation and release, toxic and calming, that I will breathe myself

into a sleep so numb I could take the first step into ankle-deep—without fear,
but knowing that beneath the surface there are bodies.

Malindi Beach

In low tide, you could walk the cove—
it comes to shoulder height

and at high tide, you have to row
your way to the outcrop of rock

where Indian Ocean crabs
try their best to stay dry,

moving from sand to boulder
as the waves rise and up

into the million crags of home.
I came here once, with my brother.

We beached our boat and floated
in nearby shallows, watching

the ephemeral fish as the hours went away
with the waves. Returning to rock,

we found our boat gone with the tide
and in the distance, rising and falling,

its blue plastic hull burst surface,
the current my brother tried to swim—

water pushing back his every stroke,
but there was nothing to be done

except watch the boat get carried away,
further and further, beyond our little

rock island, my brother's figure
slowing in the current and turning back.

I waited to ask why he couldn't outswim
the stream, why he'd even agreed

to leave the boat basking on the bar—
and as he took in each breath,

his body heaving wavelike,
the crabs appeared from the crags

of the hollowed stone, watching
our figures huddled

along the shore, waiting
for the tide to subside.

Istiklal Caddesi

I search for you, brother, in the midst of marquee light, with no eyes to see
the laughing faces circling street performers or the flashing bulbs

of sale signs saying *two scoops for two lira.* I search to find you
in the faces, not expecting yours to smile with the others, knowing

you search for something too, amid the scents of spice and roasted nuts,
revolving kebab spits, whirs and twips of toys sold on the street—

that's not why we decided to come, hours earlier, you said *let's go* and *we'll see*
Taksim late, after the protestors have gone and we made it to the edge,

saw the square empty, smaller than we'd seen on screens, and going back,
less than what we once were, we couldn't decide how to return,

whether we'd retrace our steps, or branch deeper into Beyoglu and come
upon a café or bar, take back an espresso, and keep going—

either way we exchanged more than words along a side street, and we parted,
just like we always do on trips like this, having reached a point where we

can't stand the sight of the other. It lasts only five minutes, and then we are back
searching for each other, searching in the crowds and the lights, walking

over Galata Bridge, back and forth, underneath the half moon and minaret
serenade we look for each other, at the mouth of a metro or ferry's dock

or by the swirl of traffic and towering screens—we look to say everything that isn't
sorry, that isn't an apology, if only we could meet somewhere in between.

After Two Years Traveling Abroad, Woman Found Hanging From a Tree

I can see your gaze out the window, the silences
        of a house that hasn't waked,

the straight-planed walls with interwoven leaves dancing

        wraithlike—

the pre-dawn moment when the earth lingers undecided,
        as if waiting for light

                                        or nothing at all.

You felt it too, the fear of confinement that comes after knowing
        so many cities, so many streets;

                                                        of being

tied down: the feeling that drives you into the wilderness—

        drives you to do something the others wouldn't dream.

These walls know their bounds. This land is measured, acred off.
        Even the floorboards have mouths.

Will we ever be content, you and I?

Continental Drift

Are you readying fields for rain months?
Ironing your best shirt for a Saturday morning stroll?
Are you riding a light-quick truck to the capitol packed
so tightly with others you're in no danger of being
sent flying, should the truck strike a tree or rock or carcass—
the same jolt that killed Youssouf years ago, you remember?
Are you wandering the N'Djamena streets—sea of steel doors,
untagged taxis—trying to find the home of a friend?
I'm over here—thousands of water waves away.
I'm doing the same thing: readying and not readying,
searching and not searching for you dear brother,
for you dried-up river, for you house where they cut
down the hajlij tree.
                    Did you get the message I sent—
the one wishing you a blessed Ramadan or saying I would come
if only I got a chance? Let me know you've received it—call me
across the digital divide, and let us speak in pixelated voices
a conversation we've been meaning to have, but haven't been—
for whatever reason, the line's been disconnected long ago.

Endless

I slip beneath the surface in January, so cold
the water steams from the pool into the air

like effervescent waves—

you could blow them with a breath and watch
as they take shape and sail above till they become

indeterminate from cloud.

I wish that in their airborne steam I could have a seat,
could breathe myself across borders and oceans,

breathe myself into a new skin

different than what I am now: a man, watching pool waves
lick sandstone siding, remembering

the boy who sifted grains

with his steps to join Moussa by the great road
where Toyota trucks rushed through town like zephyrs—

but now only a man, waiting

in suburbia for the myth of life to return and take him up
in its cloud one last time.

Remembrance

Here have some tea I pour him a glass *and take from the biscuit tray*
and don't forget the peanuts.

The shadows of the thorn tree twist and sickle
their way across the gravel beyond the porch—

the sky cloudless, the surrounding plain bare of life apart
from the camel train at the horizon-line

loping off toward a faraway market day.

Do you remember the time we stayed up late
                                        watching what

was the name, Sid al-Khatim—Lord of the Rings?

                                                Yes.

Well I saw it on Canal+ the other day...

Someone comes into the yard from the side gate, takes a cup of water
from the moist cooling jar in the shade.

The metal plate covering the jar's mouth rattles shut.

                                        What is it that you do now?

I work with different projects. Now, I'm with a well-digging NGO.

Yesterday, we were all the way in Ambassatna
  looking for a good place to dig.

                                                And the money?

It's all right, one day I'll save enough for a wife or maybe
just enough to move to N'Djamena

and pay the bribe to get a government job, even if it's in the South.

The wind blows from the southwest, gently enough to cool us.
Strong enough to send the falcon-shadows streaking

across the oven-sun yard.

Tell me he says *do you remember the time we watched basketball games*
and there was that short fellow, Boykins was his name—

what happened to him?

I don't know.

Tell me, why did you come back? I expected to see your brother,
I expected to see even your father.

But why you?

On the other side of the walls, a motorcycle roars to life,
then fades away along the road to town.

Ceremonial

I

When in America, I sometimes think of names,
past names and present names from a desert life—

I've heard these names between millet stalks, mud walls,
on a mat in the heat of day
heard the names along a stairway,
on a bus bussing down East-West Highway, and even heard them
on the phone coming across ten thousand miles—names like

Habib, Mht Tahir,
Sadia, Fatima, Hawa
or *Madri.*

Tell me,

how can I even begin

to think of names?

II

I think of Issa sleeping beneath the stars:
his dreams swimming in the constellations.
He is lifted up upon his mat and hovers
in the air. Beneath him, his horse raises
its head to see where its master has gone.

I think of AmGobi sitting by the empty river,
waiting for the rains to come and fill it up again.
How she holds shells in between her fingers,
drops them in the cracks that run the length
of the shoreline, in the cracks of her old skin.

I think of the little boy Moussa dancing
atop the ruins of a barracks built by the French—
he nimbly jumps from wall to wall,
jumps with the goats who have climbed
to nibble on dry nabakh leaves.

These names acquired like taste on the tongue.
These names acquired underneath the hajlij tree.

Names like Zakaria teaching a room of children,
the blackboard littered with Roman letters
and his pants dusted with chalk snow—
he teaches in the months the government bus
never comes, never brings his salary.

Like Miriam waking early at the rooster's call:
she stirs noodles into her soot-smeared pot,
slowly guiding the boiling water in a circle
before draining it, adding sweet oil
to the noodles—dweddi that slips through
your fingers and down your tongue, morning
meal as the sun rises, the cows leave town,
the beggars knock on doors for an offering.

Like Haroun, named after my own name,
born in the lantern night. I was there
at his usbu when they named him
and those around me wished their best,

and I was there when the news came
that he had succumbed to sickness.
They told me he returned and flies
among the birds.

These names have come to my ears
in between sips of tea, when you must grip
the glass at its edges or you'll burn.

These names have come softly like the sound
of brushing your feet sideways across
a sand-filled street, moving quickly
or else you'll sink.

III

From beyond names can still remain with you—
though you, if not careful, could let them flit away in thought.

Names, though in different calligraphies, span oceans,
cross borders—share the same warmth

whether from a Youssouf or a Joseph.
Zara or a Sarah.

But where can a name cross into another land, untranslatable?
When in exile, unable to return, can a name never

find its equivalent, be the very word
your mother said at birth?

Knowing only the life along the border.
Knowing no entry either to your left hand or right.

When did I cease
                    to think of names

        and begin to search

                for the sense behind them?

Here, along the border, both in dream and out, wandering for my place,
I see a thousand grains rise from days' dust-trails, rise to swirl

and skew themselves into a mirror image of myself, pleading for me
to turn, to follow the mirage of oasis in my past.

Always, I walk through the sandshadow, bursting its chest, my chest—

hearing the grains meet ground again, dust to dust,
and knowing I have once again pleaded for my end

and found only a new horizon.

IV

I press on for a place to call my own, to name with a name
that will withstand the blast of wind and desert grain.

To move in progress is to regress into the present of past
                                        to find myself

echoed in memory, rather than returned to who I once was.

My steps bring me to the shore, to the dry bed
                                        of the ephemeral river

and in its bed, I spread my arms, collecting in clenched
hands the shells of millennia, of Pangea, the fingerdust of God.

V

I might spend the rest of eternity here, along this shore,
or return tomorrow, I don't know, only I know
that when the rain comes, I will push out
into the Batha—sit there while the current
grows. I will pass by the villages and the fishers
out for only a few weeks of the year, to see
if perch have come to be caught. I will pass
by the plain opening like a book and see the cattle
streaming across its pages. I will see the mountains
of Mongo to the southeast, feel the Saharan
wind coming from the north. I will pass by all the way
to MaTabke, the place of no crying, and I will
go beyond to the lake, to find that it is several feet
shallower than last year.

Tuareg Prayer

Twenty years you waited for me to believe
in the same God as you—you, travelling
by horsecart with the rest of us, pitching
your tent next to the rainy-season-filled
pond, the gum trees sapping tears for our poverty.
We followed rain clouds. You followed us.
Showing us love. We showed you ours.

Now, as the meat on my bones passes
through death's teeth, will you remember me?
Will you, during the rainwind afternoons,
think of the date-tree shade and the tea
we shared? Will you think of our children
growing up together with the goats,
rolling bike tires with sticks
and singing to the full moon?

You have waited for me this long.
Now I ask you to hold out a little while
longer—until the millet stalks have grown
past your shoulder, and the camels come
back from the north.

Then, you too will close your eyes
one last time when the sun is at its hottest
and your belly full of camel meat.

On the other side, you will walk
the twisting path between the knife-tipped bush.
You will find me at the entrance
to the camp, waiting for you,
waiting to go in together.

Notes

The epigraphs at the beginning of this collection are taken from *The God of Small Things* by Arundhati Roy (Random House 2008), "One Art" as printed in *Poems* by Elizabeth Bishop (FSG 2011), and *Oil on Water* by Helon Habila (Norton 2011).

The song lyrics in "N'Djamena Morning" are taken from Magic System's wildly popular song "Premier Gaou."

The epigraph that begins "Memory Palace" comes from Czeslaw Milosz's "Second Space" as printed in *Second Space* (Ecco 2005).

The title of the poem "Into Another Intensity" is taken from a line in T.S. Eliot's *Four Quartets*.

Acknowledgments

My thanks to the following literary journals that have published versions of the poems below:

"After Two Years Traveling Abroad, Woman Found Hanging from a Tree" and "Batha River" in *Tupelo Quarterly*

"The Bird" in *Rock & Sling*

"Broken Oud" in *Christian Century*

"Ceremonial" in *apt*

"Communion," "Elegy," "Lake Kivu Dream," and "Teacher" in *Transition*

"Endless" in *The Curator*

"Fragment" in *CONSEQUENCE*

"Gazelle" in *RHINO*

"I don't know anything about suffering" and "The Calling" in *World Literature Today*

"Istiklal Caddesi" in *Relief*

"Jiangxi Citizens See Floating City, Phenomenon Caused by Refracted Light" in *The Cresset*

"Malindi Beach" in *Anchor*

"Maps" in *Cimarron Review*

"Memory Palace" in *jmww*

"Nasara" in *Saint Katherine Review*

"N'Djamena, Meaning 'We Will Rest'" and "Twin" in *Burningword*

"Outside Ngaoundéré" in *Literary Bohemian*

"Picture of a Family" in *Sojourners*

In addition, the poems "N'Djamena Morning," "Twin," and "Song of the Workers" have been anthologized in *Best New African Poets 2015*.

"During Kharrif" was originally published in the chapbook *Winnower* (Wipf & Stock 2013).

Unending gratitude goes out to the *subayan* of Ati, the young men who were my brothers, and to their families. Their influence and love seeps out of every pore of these poems. We have all grown up and scattered, but not a day goes by when I don't long for another glass of tea in their presence.

For friends—Nate Hansen, Siobhán Scarry, Shann Ray, William Fargason, Ruth Elizabeth Morris, Tyler Goldman, and so many others—who have at various points stepped in to provide illumination on these poems, please accept my heartfelt thanks.

To past professors, whose influence also permeates this book down to the root, thank you: Michael Collier, Stanley Plumly, Josh Weiner, Elizabeth Arnold, the late Brett Foster, and Nicole Mazzarella.

Deepest love and thanks goes to Minda, whose faith in my work and sharp eye has given life to this book and will continue to light my life.

And to you, reader, for giving your time and attention to these poems—*shukran katir.*

About the Author

At the age of eight, Aaron Brown moved with his parents and brother to Chad, where his parents did medical humanitarian work. During the ten years that followed, the crisis in neighboring Darfur and a proxy war with Sudan fueled a civil war in Chad, and Brown came face to face with this war in 2008 when hundreds of rebel trucks attempted and failed to oust President Deby in Chad's capital, N'Djamena, a battle resulting in mass casualties and decimated neighborhoods. Brown's family was evacuated to Gabon and then to France, where he spent months waiting to return. He moved back to the United States to attend Wheaton College and later to complete an MFA from the University of Maryland.

Brown has held fellowships through *Image*'s Glen Workshops as well as the Folger Shakespeare Library, and he has received Pushcart Prize and Best of the Net nominations. His poetry and prose have been published in *World Literature Today, Tupelo Quarterly, The Millions, Cimarron Review, Portland Review, Ruminate,* and *Transition,* among others. He is also the author of the poetry chapbook *Winnower* and novella *Bound,* both published by Wipf & Stock. Brown now lives with his wife, Melinda, in Kansas, where he is a professor of writing at Sterling College.

www.aaronbrownwriter.com

About the Cover Artist

Peggy Hinaekian is an American artist of Armenian origin who was born in Egypt and now lives and works in the U.S. and Switzerland. Having started painting at a young age, she is internationally recognized and has exhibited extensively worldwide. Her work figures in numerous private and public collections in the U.S. and in Europe, as well as in museums. She was the only American artist chosen to participate in the Milan International Expo in 2016 where she presented two paintings that were projected on two giant monitors throughout the Pavillon.

Hinaekian has worked as a fashion designer in Boston and New York before relocating to Switzerland where she immersed herself completely in her art. Her career evolved in stages that reflect the versatility of the different techniques and mediums used in her work. She is foremost a colorist, and it is from Egypt that emerges two of her favorite colors: the orange of the scorching sands of the Sinai desert and the turquoise blue of the Mediterranean Sea. As a color field painter who evokes the burning desert and the vast flowing seas, her paintings are best described as "Red Desertscapes and Blue Reveries." By using color and texture, she breathes movement into her abstract, atmospheric landscapes to prompt the viewer to wander into the different worlds conjured in her artwork.

Hinaekian is also an author and has published her first book, an erotic romance novel that contains illustrations of her own etchings (book website: www.OfJuliaAndMen.com). www.peggyhinaekian.artspan.com / hinaekian@hotmail.com

The interior text and display type were set in Adobe Jenson, a faithful electronic version of the 1470 roman face of Nicolas Jenson. Jenson was a Frenchman employed as the mintmaster at Tours. Legend has it that he was sent to Mainz in 1458 by Charles VII to learn the new art of printing in the shop of Gutenberg, and import it to France. But he never returned, appearing in Venice in 1468; there his first roman types appeared, in his edition of Eusebius. He moved to Rome at the invitation of Pope Sixtus IV, where he died in 1480.

Type historian Daniel Berkeley Updike praises the Jenson Roman for "its readability, its mellowness of form, and the evenness of color in mass." Updike concludes, "Jenson's roman types have been the accepted models for roman letters ever since he made them, and, repeatedly copied in our own day, have never been equalled."

The front cover typeface is Interstate. Designed by Tobias Frere-Jones in the period 1993-1999. Interstate is closely related to the FHWA Series fonts, a signage alphabet drawn for the United States Federal Highway Administration in 1949. While optimal for signage, Interstate has refinements making it suitable for text setting in print and on screen, and gained popularity as such in the 1990s. Due to its wide spacing, it is suited for display usage in print. The prize line is set in Whitney, a family of sans-serif digital typefaces also designed by Tobias Frere-Jones, originally created for New York's Whitney Museum as its institutional typeface. The back cover text is set in Fresno, designed by Jim Parkinson.

Silverfish Review Press is committed to preserving ancient forests and natural resources. We elected to print *Acacia Road* on 30% post consumer recycled paper, processed chlorine free. As a result, for this printing, we have saved: 1 tree (40' tall and 6-8" diameter), 499 gallons of water, 293 kilowatt hours of electricity, 64 pounds of solid waste, and 120 pounds of greenhouse gases. Thomson-Shore, Inc. is a member of Green Press Initiative, a nonprofit program dedicated to supporting authors, publishers, and suppliers in their efforts to reduce their use of fiber obtained from endangered forests. For more information, visit www.greenpressinitiative.org.

Cover design by Valerie Brewster, Scribe Typography
Text design by Rodger Moody and Connie Kudura, ProtoType
Printed on acid-free papers and bound by Thomson-Shore, Inc.